bridges

bridges
...an offering of hope for loss, grief and struggle

- terri st.cloud

ISBN: 978-0-9815440-4-5 (pbk)
bone sigh arts
www.bonesigharts.com
www.bonesighbooks.com

don't steal any of this work.
if you want to use it, just ask!

cover art: yohan
www.bfg-productions.com

book layout / design:
zakk and yo
www.mazuzu.com

contents

contents

ever know a boy who reminded you of tom sawyer?
i can still see that kid grinnin' at me when i was a kid.
he was even better than tom sawyer...he was andy.
one day andy was just gone. all that was there was
a horrible story of how he died. and that was it. i would
try hard not to visualize what happened to him. i'd squeeze
my eyes closed shut not to see, but that would make it
worse.....i would try hard to understand it all...and never
get anywhere...i just wanted him back in this world.

his death is the first death i recall. and one that i still think
of often. all these years later, he's still alive in my heart.
i wish i had answers, i wish i knew where andy went...
all i know is that he touched the earth and then left...and
that i have never forgotten his face.

and it is to andy that i dedicate this book.

my original intention for 'bridges' was to offer a book to people who were either dealing with the struggle of losing someone, or dealing with the grief of someone's passing that already took place. but then i started thinking... there's grief everywhere, for so many different things...and loss and dying come in millions of different shapes. and so i decided to offer this book to struggle and loss in all its forms.

i'm not a big fan of struggle. in fact, i really don't like it and go to great lengths to avoid it. when i find myself in the midst of it, i really wish it would go away. grief seems to take it to new levels that feel unbearable... and way too much to hold.

and yet...i know that some of my greatest growth....okay ALL of my greatest growth has come out of that darkness that i so want to go away.

one of my most meaningful thoughts for myself came to me as i tried desperately to find answers that weren't there. i had lost someone close to me and didn't know how to hold it. i wanted so bad to honor that person, to honor their life that they had lived, to honor their passing...to honor it all. and i just didn't know how. nothing seemed right....until it occurred to me... that if i could be the best i could be, if i could uncover my beauty inside me, and live with light, if i could become all that i am, then maybe somehow i could carry that person in that beauty.

that thought has echoed inside of me for a long time now. sometimes the sound is so faint, i barely hear it. sometimes it's loud and thunderous and i remember well and hold it close and act upon it.

i like that thought a lot. it seemed like maybe it was worth sharing.

in your struggle, losses, and grief...may you remember the light inside of you. it's always there...even when it feels so very faint....

bridges

laying bridges in place of walls,
love knows no boundaries.

for terry

she passed thru so quickly...
just long enough to make me love her.
we had only touched the surface ~
and yet, she is in my depths forever.

birth

she was telling him about giving birth~
"one of the most amazing things about it is
you have to totally trust thru the worst pain.
all you can do is release control and trust."
she stopped and stared at him.
the tears came.
"i guess that's not just during birth,
is it?" she asked, reaching for his hand.

continuing on

almost crumbling to the ground,
she stopped.
looking at how far she had traveled
and all it had taken to get there,
she recognized her strength.
the strengths she had inside of her,
the strength she had gained along the way ~
her inner power.
and so,
she stood up.
standing tall, she faced forward
and continued on.

hard times

i longed to lift the burden of your sorrow
and yet, i knew it was yours to carry.
and so i walked next to you.
side by side.
i rested when you rested.
cried when you cried.
and loved you more with each step of the road.

your struggle

it is in your struggle i see your spirit.
it is to your spirit
i give my heart.

home

her ache echoed inside of her
stirring her inner voice.
it was then that she remembered she wasn't alone~
and once again she turned inward towards home.

helen

what can i do for her?
i watch her fading in and out ~
i want to help so badly.
if i can center myself -
make my insides peaceful,
then perhaps i can share
that peace with her.

again

the time had come to let go.
again.
and once again she cried.
being gentle with her hurt
and concentrating on the good,
she reminded herself to trust.
to keep on trusting.
and once again she moved onward.

honoring them

she wept
and she ached
and she held her head.
they had died because
they had never been seen.
she felt an iron determination creep over her.
it was time to see herself -
and honor them.

echoes

the sorrow was so deep
it echoed in places that seemed untouchable.
it was to those places friends' love seeped.
so slowly and ever so gently,
their love quieted the echo.

for laura

there were no words to take the sorrow away –
but there were words to allow the sorrow to be present.
and these she offered her friend –
i will listen as long as you need me to.
and hold you longer then you ask.
who you are is who i love.
we don't need to pretend that it's all okay.
all we need to do is be.

different directions

thrown in a different direction –
overwhelmed and grieving,
she covered her face.
one by one,
they came and held her,
encouraged her
and gave her hope.
uncovering her face
and leaning on their arms,
she walked her path.

a thought

you can't let go of what you haven't held.

perhaps

perhaps power is letting go of the grip of the past
and standing empty handed facing the
future.

peace

to find peace in the darkness
and holiness in it all –
this i wish for you.

she became real

from her sorrow she found compassion.
from her grief she learned understanding.
and from her journey she became real.

open hands

she wasn't holding the sorrow.
it was holding her.
turning towards it, she opened her hands
and let it rest inside her grasp.

the holding

it's in the holding she said.
when you learn to stop letting
the pain hold you –
when you allow yourself to do the
holding –
that's when the healing is allowed
to come forth.

the sky

…and she turned to find the sky inside her.

your tears

it is your tears that run down your face,
and yet i taste their salt.
it is your hand that wipes your cheek,
and yet i feel the softness of your skin.
when you turn to face your world,
you never leave me.
you are part of me.
i am with you.

funny

funny how you could lose sight
of things so bright
she thought as she looked at the stars
all around her.
she just needed to remember they were there
she told herself
as she picked one up and held it.

in darkness

in darkness there is light.
in light there is love.
in love there is peace.

she kept going

she began to see the swirl of opposites inside her –
searing pain and tremendous love included.
focusing on the love and allowing the pain,
she kept going.

alone

alone.
surrounded by love
and yet totally alone,
the victory is up to you.
and the power is gained
in that solitary flight.

finding the door

finding the door and making it thru,
you slipped away.
while tears watered the ground,
the stars shone steadily on.

radically accept

radically accept release.
wildly desperately let go.
quietly hear the inner calm.
slowly, begin to know.

holding you close

holding you close,
my heart whispered to yours,
"i'll help you thru this.
i am with you.
you are not alone."

the whole

she could never go back and make some of
the details pretty. all she could do was move
forward and make the whole beautiful.

her cathedral

she kneeled at the cave entrance -
hands had quietly removed
the snow and ice that had blocked her view.
lit in warmth and sacredness
she gazed upon her cathedral.

the bear

you can try to feed the bear
but he will never get enough.
the best thing to do is feed yourself.

in

she was scared again.
seems she was scared a lot
these days.
time for a deep breath and another
plunge in.
it was the only way to get to where
she wanted to go.
so, in she went.

silver linings

i walked thru hell and burned my soul...
ashes falling from my hands...
part of me lost forever.
grieving,
i found the others,
burnt and charred like me.
holding on to each other,
i knew –
even hell had a silver lining.

i will not run

i will accept the falls.
embrace my scars.
live my passion.
i will not run.

a vow to my heart

i will work on the act of listening to you
and my listening abilities will grow.
i will honor those things you relay to me
and act upon them.
when i act upon them,
i will know that i am living my truth
and owe no explanations to anyone.
i will believe in your ability to accept all emotions
and will not close down to protect you.
i will direct my energies and my power
to places that will strengthen you,
not deplete you.
i will follow you in the way i wish the world
would follow you.
the child of the universe and the heart shall meld
and we shall dance as one.

what we shared

it's not about what we lost –
it's about what we shared,
and were lucky enough to hold
for a bit.
it's not about me losing you –
it's about the fact that i'll
always love you.

new day

she looked out at her new day ~
and believed again.

waves

"i don't know how to dive in and take the plunge,"
she told her friend.
"maybe it's time to sit still and let the
waves wash over you." came the answer.
her eyes filled with tears
and she knew it was true.
it was time to just release
and feel.

allowing it

it's not about controlling
it's about being present,
being open
being aware –
and allowing it to come.

just be

she suddenly saw it -
right in front of her -
she didn't have to convince anyone of
anything.
all she had to do was be.
just be.
the rest would take care of itself.

melted

the thaw began,
the ice melted
and the world opened up again.

for rachel's mom

she closed her eyes,
her tears washing her cheeks.
holding the image of the stars in her mind,
she held her daughter close
and loved her.

galaxies

did she have to drop into it?
maybe it could come swirl her away instead?
either way she had to let go,
didn't she?

unconditional

there were no conditions
with her love –
and maybe that's why
it could reach beyond
death's boundaries.

sharing it

there was talking and noise
and people trying to help.
i sat quietly reading every inch of your face -
desperately looking for a way
to take this from you.
all i could find were ways to share
it with you.
walking next to you, we'll go forward.

her treasure

the waves washed away the residue
and left her treasure.

for rachel's sister

she looked up at the nite sky
over and over again.
the stars had always twinkled so.
but now her tears mixed with her view.
and they would never be the same to her
for they had never been so precious before.

threads away

miles away?
no, threads away.
silver threads.
they're on fire today –
believe me,
i am with you.

growing

she was pleased when she saw she actually did trust.
but she had no idea how much that trust would grow.
and how strong it would make her.

wylde flower

like a flower bending in the rain –
she'd get up again
and again
and again.

splinters

she built her cathedral
from the splinters of
her shattering.

a new part

…and a new part of her journey began.

no more tears

she danced with pleasure over what
they had once had and knew that
she had been gifted with a rare treasure.
no more tears over loss.
she bowed to the universe with gratitude.

my gift

i can't rewrap my gift.

the universe opened

the universe opened and covered her with stars.

candle of peace

hold the candle of peace among the darkness
and believe.

looking up

looking up,
she saw her sky
and followed its light
out of the darkness.

forward

i can never go back.
only forward.
ever deeper.

the pain

the pain had stopped her too many times.
taking the form of fear,
it gripped her tight.
but now,
her belief became more important
than her pain.
turning towards it,
she allowed it to fill her.

reaching

in reaching beyond herself,
the empty hole shifted into a
well of possibilities.

down deep

going down deep
she screamed to the stars –
direct me!
guide me!
lead me!
pull me!
get me beyond me!
filling with their light,
she came up once more –
ready to live again.

kylie

seeing who she really was seemed to be
all that i could offer -
and so i closed my eyes.
and i saw her,
all of her.
loving her,
i released her.

her offering

unwrapping her hands
from around her heart,
she offered her all.

beams of light

beams of light stood like pillars
in the darkness.
solidly standing there
offering relief and support.
leaning into them,
she touched loved,
she touched life,
she touched meaning.

the hole

it's not so much the hole inside me that i mind,
she said.
it's the weight that's in that hole.
then take the weight out and
leave it behind and fill the hole
with things that will make you fly,
was her reply.

9/11

words can't grasp what fire can't burn.

knowing

maybe it's not about the darkness.
and maybe it's not about the light.
maybe it's about the knowing.
the knowing there is sacred always.
even when you can't see it.
maybe it's the knowing that's the
holy part.

*

more than anything

more than anything ~
i want to trust a journey
that i don't understand.

weeping

weeping and aching,
i longed to honor your passing.
i longed to honor your life.
searching everywhere,
i found only one answer.
to honor myself.
become all that i am.
and carry you inside that beauty

souls

she didn't just survive -
she became.

terri didn't know she was a writer, didn't know she was an artist, she just plain ol' didn't know a heck of a lot of anything. and then some good ol' fashioned, gut wrenching, heart ripping pain gripped her life, and she started to discover things about herself.

she began her journey inward. when the pain got to be too much for her, she spilled out her feelings on paper. wanting to honor those feelings somehow, she added art to them. it was with that mixing of spilling and honoring that bone sighs were born.

needing to find a way to support herself and her sons, she began peddling her watercolor bone sighs shop to shop. thru an amazing journey of tears, miracles, trust, terror, laughter, squeezing her eyes closed tight, and following her heart, somehow bone sigh arts became a real business.

home made books were offered for awhile among her prints and cards. cumbersome to make and lacking the desired quality, there came a time when the books needed to become "real." grabbing her sons, terri and the guys decided to go into print!

without terri's sons, bone sigh arts/books would never ever have become what it has. funny how the very reason for the business became what made the business successful. those boys are everything to both terri and bone sighs!

josh is the oldest. an old soul musician, born entertainer, and a loveable guy! yo yo is their gentle giant who's turning into the world's best graphic designer! and zakk is the logical one. computer geek and mad inventor with the marshmallow heart.

and! the boys have expanded into beginning their own businesses for themselves! (check out the information page for a listing of their websites!)

it's been quite a journey for them all.

terri's still scratchin' her head wonderin' if she'll ever figure any of it out! probably not....but she'll keep trying anyway!